S0-EIA-335

# MY TURN BIBLE STORIES ABOUT NUMBERS

## Sarah Fletcher

## Illustrated by Corbin Hillam

CPH
SAINT LOUIS

This book belongs to

..................................................................................................

# God sent 1 Baby Jesus.

Baby Jesus was born on the first Christmas.
He was God's own Son.

# He was a gift from God.

God sent Baby Jesus to save people and make them God's friends forever.
God sent Baby Jesus for you too.

# The animals went into the ark 2 by 2 by 2.

God told Noah to build the ark and put his family and the animals inside.
A big flood was coming!

# 2 by 2 by 2 they went.

The big flood came and covered all the land.
But Noah and his family and the animals were safe in the ark.
God keeps you safe too.

# Wise Men came to see little Jesus.

They knew He was God's Son.
They wanted to give Him gifts.

# The Wise Men gave Jesus 3 gifts.

One smelled good. One felt good.
And one looked pretty.
You can give Jesus a gift too—your love.

# 4 men took their friend to Jesus.

The friend couldn't walk.
So the men put him on a mat, cut a hole in the roof,
and lowered the mat to where Jesus was.

# Jesus made the man well again.

The man stood up, picked up his mat, and walked away.
Jesus helps you get well too.

# A boy had 5 loaves of bread.

He had two little fish too.
But 5,000 people were hungry.

Jesus fed all the people with that food.

And He had 12 baskets of food left over!
Jesus helps you have food too.

# God made the world in 6 days.

And what a lot God made: the sun, moon, and stars;
the land and the seas; plants, animals, and people!

# God made everything in 6 days.

God saw that His world was good.
He wants you to help take care of it.

# 7 men played 7 horns.

They marched around the walls of the city of Jericho every day.
God said they should:

# On day 7, the walls fell down.

Now God's people could go into the city.
God helps you with your problems too.

# A man had 8 fine sons.

The man's name was Jesse.
He thought his older sons were more important.

# God chose the youngest to be king.

The youngest son was David.
God knew he would be a great king—and he was.
God knows you too—and He loves you.

# 9 men did not thank Jesus.

Jesus made them well from a bad disease.
He made one more man well too.

# The last man did thank Jesus.

That made Jesus happy.
It makes Jesus happy when you thank Him too.

# A woman had 10 silver coins.

But she lost one.
So she cleaned her whole house looking for it.

# She found the lost coin, and she was happy.

Jesus said the angels are happy when one new person loves Jesus.
They are happy because you love Jesus too.

# Joseph had 11 brothers.

They didn't like Joseph.
They sold him as a slave.

# God took care of Joseph.

One day Joseph became an important man.
He saved his whole family.
God takes care of you too—wherever you are.

# Jesus had 12 helpers.

We call them Jesus' disciples.
They helped Jesus show people how much God loves them.

# They liked to help Jesus.

You can help Jesus too.
You can show and tell people how much God loves them.

# Numbers! Numbers!

The Bible is full of stories.

# So many numbers!

And the stories are full of numbers.

29

# But God sent just 1 Baby Jesus.

God had just one Son.
And He sent His Son to us.

# And Jesus saved the whole world!

Now we can be God's friends forever.
You too!

Dear Parent/Teacher:

This little book is packed with lots of learning activities for your children. First read the book to them all the way through. Let them study each picture as you go and count out the appropriate number of objects. (They'll want to count the little lambs at the bottom of each page too.)

Then let them read the book to you, using only the top line on each page. Next you can take turns, the children reading the top lines and you reading the bottom lines. It won't be long before they can read the whole book alone!

Of course the most important lesson in the book is that of God's love for the children and for all the world. Reinforce that lesson whenever you can.

The Editor